Weather Eyes

**Jean McArthur
and Linda M. Walker**

Weather Eyes

For friends who supported me through tough times
Jean McArthur

My son, Scott, died on 11 August 2020 and he is here
Linda M. Walker

Weather Eyes
ISBN 978 1 76109 675 4
Copyright © text Jean McArthur and Linda M. Walker 2024
Cover image: Jean McArthur

First published 2024 by
Ginninderra Press
PO Box 3461 Port Adelaide 5015
www.ginninderrapress.com.au

Contents

Apricot	11
Point to Point	12
Gift	13
Perfect	14
Acid	15
Remains	16
Not Yet Collated	17
Here I Am	18
Kalia	19
South	20
Fear	21
Pictures	22
Barbara	23
Into the Waves	24
Before Rain	25
Making	26
This Day	27
Good Start	28
Tsimshian Rainforest	29
Winter Solstice (21 June)	30
Weather Eyes	31
Words Together	32
Adriatic Mist	33
Boofhead	34
Wind	35
Holding Blessed Stars	36
Pink	37
What Are You	38
Sideways	39
The Middle	40

Split	41
I Sing for You	42
Hospital Quadrangle	43
Breath	44
Brittle	45
A Flash	46
Pasque	47
The Cold Comes	48
Flying In	49
About Death	50
Birds	52
Soon	53
Orchard	54
Wonderful	55
Fig Leaf	56
Plants	57
Tide	58
Tidal Vase	59
Distance	60
New Again	61
Corner Café	62
Released	63
Kimono	64
The Lover	65
Blue	66
Setting the Scene(s)	67
Summer Evening; Bushfire	68
No One Will Hear	69
Ellie	70
The Prison	71
Tree Dahlia	72
Enormous This How	73

Vicki	74
Bluey's Murder	76
Season Change	77
The Day Passes	78
Broken Crockery	79
Passages	80
Sunraysia	81
The Wondrous	82
Radio	83
He Wrote	84
May	85
What If He	86
Mum	87
She Lies on the Grass and Fans Out	88
Hush	89
Dreams	90
Bagels	91
Istanbul	92
Leaves	93
No	94
Shawnigan Lake	95
The Road to Happiness	96
Gossamer	97
Tiny Like a Fly	98
Post	99
The Red Grevillea Flower	100
Wendy	101
The Loss That Isn't Quite That	102
Frustration	103
Billythekid	104
Retired	105
He's Gone	106

Otto	107
Still	108
Larentuka to Lewoleba on Lembata	109
Hands Up	110
Mallee Rain	111
A Painting	112
Acknowledgements	113

To write you I first cover myself with perfume
Clarice Lispector, *The Stream of Life*,
University of Minnesota Press,
Minneapolis, 1989, 43

Apricot

Still warm air and a melon moon
the distant buzz of traffic
with faint cicada whirr
after a day of fearsome heat
the apricot crop is finished
warm thick orange pulp
mouth savouring, flavour lingering
balanced by cool Greek yoghurt.

Jean McArthur

Point to Point

The trees are in the street even at night with the lights out. There goes the slow stone-laden train again. The gate's closed against the wild pub crowd round the corner and the roaming squatter with his pet rosemary bush. Breathing is the most radical of occupations wrote Susan Sontag about Elias Canetti.

Linda M. Walker

Gift

Necklaces of sparkling jet
bracelets of green strands
the sea's winter gift
for smooth ochre sands.

Jean McArthur

Perfect

My first boyfriend came to visit Phyllis Knight one hot summer
Phyllis had an orange tree that needed a lot of precious water
He was perfect
Do you have anything to say he said
He wrote poems in the hammock under the nectarine tree
Now there's sea and mist and plains and hills and forests

Linda M. Walker

Acid

Five hundred kilometres, almost home –
my stomach contracts and turns.
What if it is gone?
He threatened to burn it down –
not just once.
No sign of smoke – deep breath –
acid in my throat.
What will greet me
ash or anger?

Jean McArthur

Remains

Dust rises in the distance
I have not agreed to breathe
The world includes the lotus

I rescued those three lines
As if they were remains
Of a time long gone
When someone drew
Near once again
Though absent

Linda M. Walker

Not Yet Collated

A life of fragments, scraps, shards
collected, scattered, piled, sorted
coloured paper, pictures, notes, boxes
single earrings, broken broaches
drawings, telephone jottings, books
pen lines in formation, curving, twisting
warm, worn fabrics, insects
each a history of its own
elusive when needed
inspirational when discovered
sending the mind on a journey
remembrance of person, place or time.

Jean McArthur

Here I Am

Fog rolls in and ships
        anchor out to sea
        her tiny brown mass
Takes one last breath
The grey silk dress hangs
        behind the white door
        the fire storm rolls
Across the treetops in clear view
This is how stories patch
        together bits and pieces

Linda M. Walker

Kalia

It should at least be overcast
a sombre, reverent sky.
But no, spring sunshine filters
one hundred hues
of green lush growth.
Only a few short weeks ago
bare branches laced the sky
leaves were there though
when we hugged the girl good-bye.

Happy flowers nod, smile benignly
honeysuckle air mingles
with feathered music.
I leave the absent phone
encircled in my gloom.
So soon, so young, we are not ready.
'She's coming home to die.'

Stepping into my garden of reality
sun warm on my arms
an intermittent breeze
conducts grass and leaves
in a symphonic movement.
It should at least be overcast
a sombre, reverent sky.

Jean McArthur

South

Footsteps on the stairs. A boy slumps on a chair and twists his grey jumper. He's pulling it apart. You forget he says. In the doorway a girl. She steps into the room and leans on a table crying. Then she leaves. Footsteps on the street. The call of a bird. Well says a man. A woman walks to the window. The boy jumps up and runs down the stairs. The woman leaves too. The dawn comes. The man leaves.

The steely dark slips under the glittering sky.

I sweep meat and blood-soaked sawdust off the butcher's floor and turn the lights off and lock the doors. I hang a green coat over a chair. Pollen from the pine trees falls yellow.

Linda M. Walker

Fear

Sometimes it is in my stomach
stones falling into a pit
sometimes it is in my chest
tight and terrifying
sometimes it is in my head
weather, wind, an uncertain worry
or in my throat
closing over with dread
knees quivering with apprehension.

Jean McArthur

Pictures

I weigh up the day
then wing it and find the folds
in his last sentence

I decided to stop here because I almost had an accident just as I was jotting down this last sentence, when, on leaving the airport, I was driving home after the trip to Tokyo.

There's a picture of
him as a child with jet black
hair in a toy car

And one of him with
his elbow out the window
of his father's car

Linda M. Walker

Jacques Derrida, last sentence of 'Ulysses Gramophone', trans. Tina Kendall, revised by Shari Benstock, in *Acts of Literature*, Routledge, New York, 1992, 309

Barbara

I took Doreen
to see your seaside garden
a gardening buff as well
she had battled roaring forties
then started all anew
beside an historic bluestone cottage
in Victoria's coldest parts.
I hardly got a word in
when I murmured how I'd like...
you both laughed and said
'With *your* chooks?'
Colourful coordinated plantings
artist's eyes at work.
Acre after acre of views exchanged
an entire afternoon to see it all.
Among foliage
in more established sections
elegant turquoise jar or
terra cotta mingling.
You complained of tiredness...
not surprised, I thought
of the labour all involved.
You gave us each a Chinese lantern
mine I tended carefully.
Doreen told me later
hers died inexplicably.
I sadly watched mine wilt
and wither too, then I knew
I really hope the next one
      is not you...

Jean McArthur

Into the Waves

The sky is grey
the room spins

Then she kisses him

My flat feet land soft
on the flat ground

I watch forever
his last breath

Linda M. Walker

Before Rain

Shrill excitement of New Holland honeyeaters
as they acrobat over a water pool
yellow flash, dip, and splash
a brief rest on branch above
to complete toilette, straighten feathers
pirouette for insects on humid north wind
which flutters Tibetan prayer flags
rattles bamboo Bali chimes
showers tiny white petals of agonis
fronds swaying, mini snowflakes
decorating paved veranda.
In trees beyond, urgent cicada vibrations
almost drown irregular highway traffic murmur.
Overhead tumbling grey clouds darken to indigo.

Jean McArthur

Making

The smell of
hot dry pine
sticks like glue
to my
vast plans

My two feet
carry me
like angels
making
bridges

Breath is the
blue morning
light on the
sparrows
bathing

Linda M. Walker

This Day

I need to take this day and hold it
not forever –
just until I can savour
moments of slanting sunshine
calmly casting long shadows
purple petals sprinkled on dry soil
the last coloured leaves
clinging to orchard twigs.

Trying to do so cost me
forgotten appointments
loss of credibility
dignity, money and trust.

Thready clouds wisp above
my chest hurts –
surrounded by beautiful things
I still somehow let these
moments slip between my fingers.

Jean McArthur

Good Start

Write down names and costs
and dates and times (and lies)

Suddenly a cold wind arrives
and a voice from long ago

Then a door slams

She returns and that's brave

Brown sparkling water lays
in sheets over the flats

Thunder in the distance
and grass under her feet

Linda M. Walker

Tsimshian Rainforest

Water falls gently from pale grey
only visible against dark foliage
of spruce and hemlock
sodden sphagnum swells.
Cedar shakes on roof
edges drip as I watch
silently from my window
this monochrome and
pass the shortest day.

Jean McArthur

Winter Solstice (21 June)

She was crying a woman said to another woman

The little girl slowly sipping her soup stared at me for a long time

At the airport I watched the wild weather like a hawk

Heatproof enzymes isolated from bugs brought back by (early) *Japanese drill missions* (to the centre of the earth) *are now used in washing powders*

Linda M. Walker

David Adams, 'Journey to the Centre of the Earth', in *The Guardian* (online), June 2005

Weather Eyes

I am a farmer's daughter
see the world through weather eyes
governed by irregular
rhythm of seasons
making do until the cheque…
I know the urgency of doing
before rain or heat or storm
and waiting patiently for harvest.

Jean McArthur

Words Together

When I was twelve I used
                to plan my life
                in the evenings
                while the rain fell
                month after month

Then he died and
                tonight the
                house shakes

                there's banging
                at the door

One word then another word
                petals flutter
                rivers flow
                autumn leaves scatter
                bugs chirp and susurrate
                lovers meet and part
                moons wax and wane

Linda M. Walker

Thomas Lamarre, 'Diagram, Inscription, Sensation', in *A Shock to Thought, Expression After Deleuze and Guattari*, ed. Brian Massumi, Routledge, London & New York, 2002, 150

Adriatic Mist

I am such a nothing person – steel-blue amongst sage-green
I who love nature – all growing things – except weeds –
I don't hate weeds – just plants in the wrong place…
I who love all living things – except crocodiles and snakes –
not hate exactly, a dislike of harmful things – that includes you.
Venomous words and scarlet accusations –
assumptions of your correctness.
A total disregard for others' position or feelings –
out of step – out of place – out of time.

Jean McArthur

Boofhead

I won't rubbish
my hundred husbands

I was always too old and
they were always too young

One called the other
boofhead

Fair enough too

Linda M. Walker

Wind

How can I draw the wind?
Especially this wild, wild wind
thrashing bushes and shrubs
tossing casuarina's hair
whispering in her ears
moaning intermittently along
eaves and window cracks
as though in constant pain.

Jean McArthur

Holding Blessed Stars

End gentle hands soon and then you
Turn your earth under the red blow
All this time nowhere quite as forever cold
Hear the sirens over the sacred heart fire
And the wind in sharp sigh notes
What you look like was way to forget
The small bones in his arms by any other name
As from a short fall and it's still early days
Put the same shoes on shout to hours
The small blue bird with his white sails

Linda M. Walker

Pink

I am not a pink person.
Why do you give me flowers of pink?
I am yellow, from sharp lemon
through to harvest gold
with orange around the edges
and fading to rusty brown.

Jean McArthur

What Are You

I'm like
        a likeness of me
        unlike you who
        oozes you

I laughed, 'Why do I need roses
with their sharp thorns?' He asked,
'What can I do then,
if I am so in love with you?'
I got annoyed: 'Stupid!
What are you?' I asked, 'A prince?'

You did not bring me
        white roses or
        daffodils or
        pebbles

No thoughts either

And I made a little fuss
        in my pearl
        necklace

Linda M. Walker

Anna Akhmatova, 'By the Sea Shore', in *Selected Poems*, Penguin Books, London, 1969, 62/63

Marianne Moore in her poem 'I've been thinking' begins, 'Make a fuss / and be tedious', in *Selected Poems,* Faber and Faber, London, 1969, 75

Sideways

My sights are not set on the goal, but on the journey
or if the mind was focused, I was distracted on the way
by colours, shapes, aromas, conversations
the flutter of wings startled from a bush
some aspect high-lighted in a certain season
intricate lacework of cobwebs in a normally unlit corner
slight feather adjustments of birds balancing on a wire
or symmetry of a pelican or eagle soaring high above.

Jean McArthur

The Middle

Tiny lights glowed and a tall tower was stark against the sky.
A woman stood on a houseboat looking at misty mountains.
A man put his arm around me and talked about escaping.
I heard a voice quietly say 'according to the stars'.
On a beach smooth pebbles washed up with a clinking rhythm.

A ripple like a breeze crossed the ground and closed a door.
An apple-shaped shadow quivered in a warm corner.
The corner boldly stared at me for everyone to see.
Not knowing life could be like this I vanished.
A tree nearby rustled when a crow landed on a high branch.

Linda M. Walker

Split

On separation –

A day of tears
A day of bribery
A day of wheedling
And declarations of love

– Not necessarily in that order.

Jean McArthur

I Sing for You

I sing for you
>and you do not sing for me

Birds sing for you
>and you do not sing for them

Nevertheless, a storm can distract your attention. Your attention becomes the rasping noise of a stick drawn across the edge of a bowl at a party. It draws attention tenuously from your fingers, the way your body starts to hurry in the wind.

Linda M. Walker

Mei-mei Berssenbrugge, 'Alakanak Break-Up', in *I Love Artists, New and Selected Poems*, University of California Press, Berkeley, 2006, 31

Hospital Quadrangle

Enclosed by wards and lulled
by air conditioners' hum
we wait for tests and evaluations
with others breathing air
free from antiseptic aromas
and medical announcements.
Water slowly trickles into layered ponds
surface almost covered in maple shapes
of brown and gold and buff and ochre.
Rocks hold rushes to fringe
green edges of the stream.
Now and then a hissing in branches
high above sends more shapes
sailing, drifting, twirling, down to
obscure a little more bright reflection.

Jean McArthur

Breath

Scent of jasmine
Brown chimney tops
      through the window

Loud pounding in my ears

Breath for the child
      who is leaving

Linda M. Walker

Brittle

I cannot break today
there simply isn't time
clear pale sky, cold green sea
thrashes foam on golden sand
surrounded by scraps of seaweed
ocean's winter debris
Monday's sun belies
August's season making
more brittle the debris of my life
…my trembling hands
and brain *must* firm
within one hour
the wringing of my insides
must calm to let
the sclera dry…

Jean McArthur

A Flash

I'll stay
six hundred and six years
you said

Roof creaks in wind

No comes in a flash

We were not birds
who collect soft weeds
to ease each other

Linda M. Walker

Pasque

It is cold.
A chill breeze whispers through dark fir trees behind me
and tosses the tow-haired stalks of spent anemones.
They mass until the distance is a blurry shivering carpet
Bleached – fading to the still silent forest
and yet another indigo mountain…
Their hair, stiffened, all swept to point the same direction
toward the ruffled lake frothing at its edges.

Jean McArthur

The Cold Comes

Howling spreads
in the starlight
like smoke

A million frogs
and still no truce

She looks you
in the eye
cold sober

Hands over ears
breath sucked in

Words be
come dust

Linda M. Walker

Flying In

Down and through fog-like clouds
        we emerge into harsh sun glistening
on dark forest squares and rectangles
        ochre triangles blend to tufted paddocks
of buff winter grass softening.
        Flags, clotheslines, windsocks flutter
colours tangling, smoke-grey sheep
        stirred soil combed and magpies
wooden frames creep away from houses
        farms protrude from sheoak scrub
mottled cattle muddied puddles
        dams rippled by coots, waterhens
panic paddling from us swishing overhead
        and bump to land.

Jean McArthur

About Death

#1

Gentle sweet air blew round the bared heads in a whisper, wrote Joyce in Ulysses (somewhere in the copy John gave me). A ninety-mile beach. Swarms of tiny black flies. Stink of rotting shrimp. Blue sky, white clouds, mist. Passing Lake Albert. Someone mentions 'scales' and 'mullet'. Nora died before I was one.

#2

Two men at dawn wake us for *transporting north to the big smoke*. It's the Queen's Birthday. Bumping along the road to Kingston. Might see the pelicans. And the brown foam along the shore. Tradition comes with change, says one of the men. It comes in the middle of the night, says the other one. Then a long conversation about gout. Many newborn lambs. Jonquils. Ghost gums in the paddocks. Piles of white stones. The army in camouflage vehicles with long aerials, lights blazing, head south.

#3

Coorong scrub. Should tell the child all the bushes and grasses and stones and birds and rabbits and rain are inside her. It's not raining now though. The blue sky is getting closer. A ferry, two blue wrens, two palm trees, four willow trees, five windmills, a river, bamboo. Truly rural, I hear. White horse, cross your feet, I hear. A crop of soursobs. Smoke in the distance. An alpaca farm. Lake Alexandrina. Black swans. A man beside a fence in a lime green jumper. *Turtles crossing the road* written on a signpost. The Finnis River. We talk about our mothers' deaths.

Linda M. Walker

Birds

Friends hiding in the fig tree heed not the distant roar of traffic
silver-rimmed eyes peer from behind leaves between mouthfuls.
A little rain and then sun opened the fruit nicely for honeyeaters
who sup then wheel and acrobat for passing insects.
Because I sit here starlings left and posted sentries for when I go.
Sparrows are bolder but wary and use the opposite side of the tree.
Wattlebirds large and speckled grey ornamented only
with scarlet earrings eye me cautiously as they eat.
Kumquats already glowing lush yellow against deep evergreen
and the loquat tree's huge dark crinkled leaves where
the birds will move to claws of sweet blossom in due course.

Jean McArthur

Soon

And so on and

Four syllables
Three spaces
And if the middle
Space withdraws
So does a syllable

So on is *soon*

And soon and

And as soon as

And it soon became clear

And (as) soon as day breaks

And so on and

Sunshine and grass and fig trees and roads and birds and forests and roses in the gardens of friends and daisies and poppies and the dream of the little dog chasing a fox and sunflowers flattened by the wind and green apples on an apple tree and moths around the outside light at midnight and the purple flowers of the veronica and the magpies singing at dawn and

Linda M. Walker

Orchard

When I bought this place, there were five apple trees
weeds, debris from dogs, peach, lemon, feijoa and plum
cooking all from Germanic heritage
childhood farm life and Canadian tutoring.

Evolution of house and yard took fruit trees
peach first, then apples one by one
as codling ate the marriage
adding cherry, persimmon and nectarine.

A plethora of lemons always blemished skins
preserved, hot and sour, warm lemon tart – slightly bitter
the more prolific the lemon, the sourer the marriage
    – so they say.

Jean McArthur

Wonderful

The dark is immense
and falls easily on my head and feet
I say the word w o n d e r f u l
        and years pass and trees quietly die
The small grey cat is lonely now I'm
        a grain of sand a hover fly a mustard seed
The pages of a thin book are
like plums or grapes or lakes

Linda M. Walker

Fig Leaf

Above the urgent buzz of traffic
I heard a leaf fall
large lobed and yellow

it met obstacles of
others, more green, slid slightly
scraping its roughness
onto a branch, almost bouncing

a rustle, a whisper
then silently rested among
the hellebores awaiting their turn
to smile and nod when
limbs above have bared.

Jean McArthur

Plants

By law plants should
be written into every line
as c(l)ues

On the one hand...
the day's too hot to
dig potatoes

Waves break against
the slowly melting
limestone cliffs

On the other hand...
wattle seed pods spin
and loudly crack open

Writing is (nothing but)
deep roots turning
        inside out

Linda M. Walker

Tide

I will not give up
        abandon myself to
wild erratic sobs
        as the sea flings
itself to thrash the sand
        the jellied heart
the quivering gut must
        abate with the tide
gather deep into its ocean
        strength set with steady
hands, logical thoughts
        to shift the sand
grain by grain

Jean McArthur

Tidal Vase

look at world weather
look at stretch of coast
look at snowflake
plainly it can't be done
need instead a lever
of monstrous length
or a remarkable man
like Pierre-Simon Laplace
the founder of tidal theory
(and spherical harmonics)
embrace he said the great bodies
and the tiny atoms
and especially the eye
and a simple sweet airstream
over the reef on a summer day
and a tiny elegant airstream too
blissful and bell-shaped
on a bright cool day

Linda M. Walker

Distance

The sun not yet up
a scarlet sky
plump moon shadow
hung in the west.
Autumn day warmed
slowly picking figs
planning letters to friends
who accepted me
for just being myself.

The distance fills my throat.

Jean McArthur

New Again

For many days I was silent, I became tired. A night sky fell on me, I bought flowers from the shop on the side street.

Then a sentence from an old book was new again. *Waiting is an enchantment: I have received orders not to move.*

Linda M. Walker

Roland Barthes, *A Lover's Discourse, Fragments*, trans. Richard Howard, Hill & Wang, New York, 1987, 39

Corner Café

Convenient for warm lunches
tea and cake within the budget
of older folk, part time or pensioners.
Old coats, worn shoes
no need to dress in style.

New green chairs brighten
upgraded menu – higher prices.
Instead of warming winter grey
cold green chairs
bring a cut in clientele.

Jean McArthur

Released

he is old as trees
in the pitch black

he has few charms
and a cruel tongue
that will kill him

yet driving home fast
along the coast road
after being set free

he sees red leaves
and bright green ferns

Linda M. Walker

Kimono

From forgotten drawer
black rayon slides on fingers
kimono wrap slinky
self-patterned, a flower perhaps
embroidered junk sails
of variegated pink
scuds across the back
flying gulls encircle.
Hong Kong gift from
foreign admirer passing
through that city
and my life.

Jean McArthur

The Lover

He bought silk in Benares
so fine as to be weightless
and in two days an Indian
tailor had made her a dress

In the long run
writers only serve their
demons she said loudly
moving in soft grey

Linda M. Walker

Han Suyin, *The Mountain is Young*, Jonathan Cape, London, 1958, 303

Blue

Mosque domes under Persian sun
    In Isfahan, Bukhara
        And walls in Samarkand
Medicinal blue through an
    Apothecary's window
        Refracting generations
Blue velvet tropic nights
    Deep blue cord dress
        Cream lace pocket trim
Sunlight sapphire shards
    Old family fragments
        Forgotten Flinders farm
Blue glass, rich, translucent
    A bowl, a jug, a tiny dish
        To hold pretend food for
Some small stuffed Egyptian donkey
    Grey war present
        From a doting uncle
            Filled with shrapnel.

Jean McArthur

Setting the Scene(s)

the morning was cold & misty / twelve soldiers
stood at ease / three cars drove slowly toward
them & stopped / from the middle car stepped an
old man, a middle-aged woman, her hair streaked
with grey & drawn into a bun, and an elderly nun /
the two women, holding hands, walked to a solitary
leafless tree / they exchanged a few words / the
nun turned & walked back to the cars, leaving the
other woman by the tree / she tucked a wisp of
hair back under its pin / she waited / she waited /
she / the officer raised his sword / the soldiers
fired / an army surgeon stepped forward to
deliver the *coup de grâce* / he looked at the figure
against the foot of the tree / she had refused to
be bound or blindfolded / it was six-eleven / she
was taken to the dissecting room of a nearby
hospital where her body was used for
medical science / she had loved soldiers

Linda M. Walker

Summer Evening

Fleet swallows soar, sink
and circle on the insects'
tropic wedding night.

Bushfire

Hot gusts of north wind
bring eucalyptus smoke haze
and strange yellow air.

Jean McArthur

No One Will Hear

These red sunsets
        lead to winter

How did I once
        save the forest

I'll know soon enough
        when talk runs out
        and moths return

        and footsteps
        (outside)
        (late)

Meanwhile we can
        visit the green parrots
        drunk in the pear trees

Linda M. Walker

Ellie

Why didn't I try to contact you again?
I knew it would be rough for you
that first year or so.
I did phone once, your Mom
gave me your address
but I never followed through…
I was thinking of vegetables
you stepped into my mind
we ate well when I visited
lonely from next door.
You taught me ice hockey intricacies
while Ria was at work
you had endless time
dangling on a bureaucratic string
intending to begin your dedication
– never did.

It all went horribly wrong.
Your lover dosed up on insulin
just to keep you there.
We loitered in psychiatric wards
until they sent her home to Africa.
Ria had found you feeding mice
in a bare Johannesburg room.

Jean McArthur

The Prison

a long white cloth floats high
in the sky as I pass the pink
rose vine on my way to visit the
steel cell with the big sliding bolt
next to the police station behind the
dentist beside the butcher and the
baker and across the road from the
post office and the grocery store and the
football oval and down the road from
the timber mill and the pine forests

Linda M. Walker

Tree Dahlia

Our world is wet with soaking surface rain.
The sky is jubilant, clean leaves glisten
but underneath, it has not healed
nor yet erased
the scars of lengthy drought.

Petals of delicate mauve
strew darkened ground
others drooping cling
to yolk yellow centres.
Sparkling teardrops
dangle from their tips
brilliant against indigo.

Jean McArthur

Enormous This How

I am in hand until back in room
And the black everything was as I'd left it
Midnight pots held dead ferns
And a washing machine
With torn shirts and towels
Plastic chairs
In the background more dark
Flush windows between
And take off the sky rain was
A dismal sight far in the distance
Of hope would carry me to those peaks
Was playing waltzes these said
He went on to recite the lyrics
Showed a procession of heads
Crowds this lovely gliding
More precise more disturbing
The windows I moved to an armchair
I dozed and dreamed the life I lived

Linda M. Walker

Vicki

As I passed the Warrumbungles
I thought of times we
had shared in seventy
with trips, picnics and the like.
At work, you the student, I the teacher
in our rooms with Nicky at the guitar.
Or visiting Lorraine and Des
in their modern block of air.
Remember Hill End
with ghosts a century old
communal cows, a flock of geese
and blackberries?
We ate them rich with cream
that night beside our campfire.
We found hidden places
Glen Davis aglow with sunset fire
the end of a magic road.

New Zealand two years later
we toured from top to toe
growing fat with relatives
absorbing autumn air.
An aqua Clutha River
flowing past our carpet floor.
Milford's eerie mists, thin high falls
Homer Tunnel and Te Anau Au.
Dolphins escorting us
through the Bay of Islands.
Cape Rienga, sea birds in salt spray
from the bus along the beach.
We farewelled from shipside
and would never meet again.

Jean McArthur

Bluey's Murder

The plan was to pay Bluey the hitman $500 to kill Mr A
Mrs A's counsel reckons Bluey's a figment of Mr L's imagination
Mr L was the local butcher and Mrs A's lover

Bluey's missing and people worry they've eaten him

In sandhills we find a tooth and a small glass bottle with a red top
We put the tooth in the bottle and throw it in the ocean

Linda M. Walker

Season Change

This morning yellow sunshine
sparkled on infant green velvet.
Clean leaves refreshed
after long drought
were dancing in the breeze.

Orchard tatters cling
scarlet, crimson, yellow, rust
fluttering against pale grey
accentuating hues.

On bare persimmon branches
only orange orbs
and one or two sparrows
searching for a soft spot.

Jean McArthur

The Day Passes

1. The palm tree won't blow over

2. The sentence 'you are mad' rings like a bell

3. A car speeds past and the geranium leaves glow in sunshine

4. The screeching gulls the dripping tap the roaring fire make a sound wave

5. I'll move to the plains when my bones wear thin

Linda M. Walker

Broken Crockery

Arrayed along the bench
        not yet in rows
                all upright – separate
In patterns of the past
        hardly two the same
                each piece holds a lifetime
of scars to tell its history
        – chips, cracks, mends
                they're still useable.

She, about to move to where
        help was close at hand – in case
                offered me these gifts
Precious ties to times ago
        and people dear now gone –
                I understood but couldn't.
Remembered patterns but
        not the stories or the people
                and she knew every one.

Jean McArthur

Passages

Please throw away everything including gloves scarves socks shirts and frocks

He's smoke and mirrors and says he's worn out by hours and days and weeks and months and roaming animals and plants

On my lap is a book and its small words like *slowly* and *whereupon* and *climb* and *pardon* and *obey* float up on this summer night and burst like bubbles

Linda M. Walker

Sunraysia

Grey-green mallee eucalyptus
lignum and spinifex tangles with
shorts, prickly memories of sunshine
of laughter, fears, hopes and tears
deep brown river eddying
cold, caressing, luring
endless oranges, sweet sultanas
open sunny people and places
dry rusty Arumpo Road sand
whirr of wheels, a velvet-green car
cigarettes, coffee and Walpeup wipe-out
block pruning, pulling out, rolling on.

Pink Lakes, Psyche Bend and Spider's Web
in a house with no interior walls.

Jean McArthur

The Wondrous

In a small dark room
cold with fever
and Paris streets
and pine forests
and Djuna Barnes
you'll want to know
the time of day
once in awhile
for the warmth
of the wondrous
a white
silk scarf
a silver
bracelet
scarlet
gloves

Linda M. Walker

Radio

He had already requested her departure
both going through motions until
such time – silent winter lunch.
Radio documentary of divorce
causes, reasons, citing samples
'Mental cruelty', voice droned on…
Eyes locked, mute recognition
realisation. At the end
'You'd never prove it'
was all he said.

Jean McArthur

He Wrote

If I'd listened more closely
>to George
>perhaps I'd have
>heard him say
>that Marianne Moore
>grew wings

>slowly at first

>>atom by atom she
>>became a blue
>>black dragon

She took to the sky
Hell-bent on making a stir

I would have liked to
>*speak to you for hours*
>*about the hour…*
>he wrote

But he didn't

>>>>>*Linda M. Walker*

Marianne Moore wrote a poem called 'O To Be a Dragon' ('of silkworm size or immense'), *Selected Poems*, Faber & Faber, London, 1969, 57

Jacques Derrida, 'The University Without Condition', in *Without Alibi*, trans. Peggy Kamuf, Stanford University Press, Stanford, 2002, 228

May

The fog lasted a long time today.
Hung about till ten, softening, muting
dulling dampening diffusing
making it difficult to get out of bed.

A breeze sprang up dispersing
banishing all traces to the horizon
drying the soil a little more
whispering secrets to the south

coercing coloured leaves to fall
luring yellow and crimson
to dance among grasses and
quivering pussy-tail heads to nod.

Warm autumn sunshine pale blue sky
sighing casuarina needles sway languidly
black-faced cuckoo-shrikes forecast rain.
What do they know? Do they really know?

Jean McArthur

What If He

warrior bones align
cells burn brittle
tall orange buds
glow on rocks
ancient arrows
pierce the trees
here it comes
here it comes
wings spread
the beloved
shadow passes
then asters
and rain

Linda M. Walker

Mum

Our Mum,
Whose mother died the day she was born
scorned and bullied by her stepmother

Our Mum
Who lived most of her life with outside toilets
searches corridors in the night

Our Mum
Who always dried laundry by stove or open fire
tried to dry undies in a microwave

As we pack her things, my sister and I
Our Mum at 89 says
'I'll try to be a good girl'
We turn away and mumble reassuring words.

Jean McArthur

She Lies on the Grass and Fans Out

Her skin peeled off and was swept into a corner

Her birth took more time and energy than was expected

Her big black wings were made of many delicate folds

Her supple limbs and large grey eyes were not blessings

Linda M. Walker

Hush

Hush
      Listen
to the lilting call of the loon
      reverberating across a lonely lake
echoing from silent spruce on sombre shores

Jean McArthur

Dreams

Together the men and the women paused

In the street stood a shiny object struck by lightning

It was a very serious moment

Then the men and women lurched forward as if their bones were loose, as if they had forgotten how to walk

Later I dreamed a rhinoceros cornered Richard, he was waving his arms, trying to keep it at bay, its skin was silvery brown, suddenly it jumped like a rabbit and charged him, he was knocked down and his head disappeared into its mouth, I threw stones and it loosened its grip, a woman arrived who said she'd call the police, and then more people arrived and I saw the back of Richard's head, the rhinoceros was still, then the dream ended…

Linda M. Walker

Bagels

I was making Bagels – it took longer than I thought.
Boiled – half-baked when my guest arrived.
'How did you know' she asked, 'that I was Jewish?'
I didn't, it was by chance.
We sipped afternoon coffee on the sun porch.
Circular wooden table, three smooth river stones
carefully centre placed, fading red lines painted
by a friend from Akhalkalaki, in the Caucasus.
Blue convolvulus clambered over wooden fence.
Hot bagels with jam of huckleberries picked
at Shawnigan Lake last month.

Jean McArthur

Istanbul

Thunder rolled wind howled windows shook

In a shoe shop a man waiting for his size to arrive said that twenty-five years ago in Istanbul on his way to the border he saw a woman dressed exactly like me and in reply i showed him my bag with ISTANBUL stitched on the front

I'll see you again he said with new shoes

Linda M. Walker

Leaves

In the sullen morning
        sodden brown leaves
                lay in drifts and heaps
yellow, red or burgundy shapes
        occasionally punctuate poignantly
                and I with unborn tears wade through
viciously, deliciously
        kicking the dying mass
                as a child would
scattering shapes.
        The sky has cried for me
                after Saturday evening's tempest
lightning flashes and much angry thunder
        a dramatic exit followed.
        And I, the silent one,
now collect the scattered leaves of life
        repositioning to fit
                however temporary.

Jean McArthur

No

She draws a blank no no one knows. She takes a firm grip as if to stand. No no no that's not a sign. Sand in her eyes no harm done. Sun the next day and the next day. Skin cracking on elbows and heels. A tiny split in the sky opens her eyes. She is here by the cows and the hills. From the porch white smoke at midday. A surprise call no a small worn voice. No she has changed her mind. No small matter.

Linda M. Walker

Shawnigan Lake

At Shawnigan Lake we picked huckleberries
in dappled sunlight through the leaves above
– an understorey day.
On the drive home she said, 'You look so much better.'
I was startled. What could she see?
What did she see six weeks ago?
Was I so transformed? What had changed?
No matter, it was an understorey
I was not yet ready to reveal…

Jean McArthur

The Road to Happiness

I'm up north walking through dry creek beds

Look at the ripples on that rock she says it was at the bottom of the sea and look there's a carving of a man holding a spear 10,000 years ago

On the hill a new pine forest is beginning all by itself

Someone yells 'I can't believe the weather'

In the kitchen back at the house another woman makes churros and talks of chocolate as the road to happiness

Linda M. Walker

Gossamer

Yesterday the sky was white
still, sulking, holding its breath
orchard leaves of brown
orange, yellow, a hint of red
scatter on the earth.
Today is so clear you
can see into infinity
blue, paled and tempered
by whips of filmy cobwebs
drifting ethereally –
gossamer of
erigone or cyclosa.
From where did they come?
Where will they go?
To begin new lives where
grass is always greener?

Jean McArthur

Tiny Like a Fly

I should not be bored (in this room of dying)

…which is tiny like a fly…passing clouds…pass…and i should not be bored in this room without a book…what tree is that over there…not a leaf left…the next moment comes…the next moment comes…an Apache rose in winter sun…don't mention Jackson Pollock or Gerhard Richter…don't mention my name or the moon…who goes there banging metal on metal…i should not be bored…

Linda M. Walker

Post

I am a grey fence post stringing up the wild Chilcotin slopes
leaning now, held only to my compatriots by two loosening wires.
Once there were four tight wires, we stood straight, proud and brown
fresh from lodge-pole pines. Winds of time have smoothed sharp edges
moss has softened my leeward side, adding rich green.
The west is weathered by winter's snow, summer's sun
       and rubbed smooth by passing deer.

Jean McArthur

The Red Grevillea Flower

The tall dog cries in long sharp yowls
At the first sign of disaster my legs give way
The house is blood and bones and *that's that*
Being old I teach myself to breathe slow like a frog
I'm the honeyeater hanging from the red grevillea flower

Linda M. Walker

Wendy

Wendy in New Guinea
>have I lost you forever?
You never answered when I wrote
>after years of silence.
Lost your address –
>I told you that.

I loved your wit
>English quips,
your sudden smile and laugh.
>Remember the day
you, Christina and I
>went to find a tree?

Shared meals in Nurses' Home
>trips south or east.
How fair and thin you were
>after a central illness –
healthier years later when
>we toured Cornwall and Devon
drank mead in English pubs.

You told me he was not for me
>I didn't heed your words
I'd like to see you one more time
>tell you, you were right
but most of all to hear your voice
>and see your smiling face.

Jean McArthur

The Loss That Isn't Quite That

All kinds of bad thoughts surface / it's the land of grief / who will come to stay who is here already who will heat the milk / have i seen you lately / am i stopping time am i running away / i should put my glasses on stay inside / it's impossible it's impossible / it's possible i can't do this it's possible words will make things worse and i'll be stung by what words would do if i was someone else and i'm not and i'm lost in the loss that isn't quite that but is too if i'm true / so airily i do my job and walk below the earth and recall a shop and food with tight skin that today is even tighter and a drop of water in a deep cut on the table that I thought would vanish in a second is there an hour later / a door closes with a grating sound

Linda M. Walker

Frustration

My father took any anger or frustration of the times
to the paddock where he attacked the yaccas
and the rabbit plague hiding there
grubbing out a few of the many
fibrous roots clinging to thick black soil.

In later years he left them to shelter new
born lambs beneath their skirts
creamy flower spikes to feed the bees
and us when the bee man came to leave his hives
and a drum of honey for our pantry.

I took any anger or frustration to the wood heap
where tough and gnarly gum logs
refused to split – only chips flew off my axe
which swung malevolently
fuel for our bathwater at least.

Now any anger or frustration goes down on paper
names changed to protect the innocent
even if it is eventually shredded.
I wield my pencil with retorts and revenge
satisfied by punishment enough.

Jean McArthur

Billythekid

How's your old man he said, i didn't know who he was, my father said it's Billy, i can see you now i said, i wrote down that he called my father your old man, my father had never been my old man i'd never called him my old man i'd never thought of him as my old man, my father heard him say how's your old man, he was right there on a chair beside me waiting to see a doctor, Billythekid was waiting to see a doctor too, I hadn't seen Billythekid for forty years, i won't know him if I see him again, my father won't be there to say it's Billy

Linda M. Walker

Retired

Walking everywhere
him to get the morning paper
join the National Trust, to try his hand
at rolling balls along the grass
and assimilate with locals.
She rejected balls when they said
to keep her hemline to the rules.
She returned the uniform
stayed home and wrote a book.
Together they explored scrub
to label every plant
stroll along the windy shore
with dotterels and oystercatchers
or drive the saline lake edge
where migratory shorebirds feed.

Jean McArthur

He's Gone

Small words, like poppy seeds, dew drops, snowflakes, slow down and slip by unnoticed. What was he doing in the library, day after day, circling like an eagle, was he looking for love or a book about love. Now he's gone away again, just when the Monarchs arrive, and the difference between *the earth tinily whirls* and *anything else uncanned* (to quote e.e. cummings) is a garden for the birds.

Linda M. Walker

Otto

Made for each other
but not the way you thought.
I think we were
for at that time
both our souls were scarred.

We needed a friend
who would accept
the way we were
to clamber to our feet again
face the world once more.

We could not share our souls
they were too bruised to air
needed time, space to heal
then protection from
another unexpected assault.

Had we met another time
maybe brief conversation
is all we would have shared
because, even at our best
we both remain reserved.

Had we met another time
our souls may have joined
with Germanic heritage.
Your gentle humour, like my Nan's
had the power to make me smile.

Jean McArthur

Still

I'm a little fed up
Let's say
With things
This and that
Stuff
More stuff
Tidying
Forgetting
(Remembering)
Falling in love
Notbeingfalleninlovewith
Again
Is it enough to
Think of a painting
Forever
Is it enough for life
I mean
And then there's the
Recipe for Anzac Biscuits
With wattle seeds
And I just wish
People would stand
       Still

Linda M. Walker

Larentuka to Lewoleba on Lembata

Hand loaded cargo
wooden ferry swaying
chugs slowly, sliding through
ultramarine waters, placid, rippling
hot canvas shields stinging sun
passengers settle to talk, play cards
sidle up to strangers to see
what they are reading, drawing
a dictionary conversation.
Ocean a mass of tiny peaks
navy deep and dark stretching
to verdant islands a mile away
smouldering mountain peaks
puff cloud into cerulean sky
encircled in a world of
volcanic blue – a ring of fire.
I blink and stare in awe.

Jean McArthur

Hands Up

I walk fast in the quiet cool night
and talk to the man with oysters

I write one hundred thousand times

I must say nothing I must say nothing
I must go nowhere I must go nowhere

Happily a red dahlia opens

Linda M. Walker

Mallee Rain

Opaque sky, weeping endlessly
Rusty sands soaking, absorbing
Slowly greening low hills
Many armed mallees
Stoically sipping, sharing
with bushes beneath.

Jean McArthur

A Painting

corner to corner
dots cones diamonds
and they're global
like Sophie Taeuber is

the poison green
the spray of golden ink
the fabric petals stuck on
the bare tree by the blue lake
the scraps of letters D A U K S
the rough black stripes on purple

a painting of a southern land
with everything *quite* there

Linda M. Walker

Acknowledgements

The following poems by Linda M. Walker were previously published:
'About Death' a version in *Otoliths*, Issue 54
(the-otolith.blogspot.com), 2019
'Released' in *The Crow*, Ginninderra Press, June 2020
'Setting the Scene(s)' in *Landfall*, Volume 46, Number 2,
Christchurch, 1992, 162
'No one Will Hear' in *tamba*, The Goulburn Valley Writers
Group Inc., Issue Number 70, 2022, 43
'Enormous This How' a version in *Thresholds* (chapbook),
Trainwreck Press, Canada, 2022, 3
'What If He' in *The Crow*, Ginninderra Press, December 2022
'No' a version in *Otoliths*, Issue 67
(the-otolith.blogspot.com), 2022
'The Loss That Isn't Quite That' in *Otoliths*, Issue 63
(the-otolith.blogspot.com), 2021

We wish to thank Stephen Matthews of Ginninderra Press
for saying yes to our manuscript (a joyful day),
and Jude Aquilina for her kind words
and endless encouragement.

www.ingramcontent.com/pod-product-compliance
Lightning Source LLC
Chambersburg PA
CBHW070119110526
44587CB00015BA/2363